CYTOLOGICAL VARIATIONS IN THE BLOOD AND BLOOD-FORMING ORGANS OF WHITE-FOOTED MICE EXPERIMENTALLY INFECTED WITH TRYPANOSOMA CRUZI

BY

SHERWIN F. WOOD

University of California Publications in Zoölogy

Volume 41, No. 26, pp. 389–418, plates 20–22

Issued October 8, 1937

Price, 50 cents

University of California Press
Berkeley, California

―――――

Cambridge University Press
London, England

CYTOLOGICAL VARIATIONS IN THE BLOOD AND BLOOD-FORMING ORGANS OF WHITE-FOOTED MICE EXPERIMENTALLY INFECTED WITH TRYPANOSOMA CRUZI

SHERWIN F. WOOD

INTRODUCTION

INVESTIGATIONS of Ezequiel Dias (1912), Mazza (1926a,b), Geoghegan (1929), Niño (1929), and Naegeli (1931) have shown that a lymphocytosis is characteristic of infections with *Trypanosoma cruzi* Chagas, the causative agent of Chagas' disease. The present study was undertaken in an effort to determine what significant changes are produced in the cytology of the blood and spleen of mice experimentally infected with the recently discovered California strain, and whether these agree with the above-mentioned investigations. The writer's findings confirm the conclusion of Kofoid and Donat (1933a, b, c) and of Wood (1934a, b) that the parasite occurring in California is *Trypanosoma cruzi*.

The author wishes to express appreciation to Dr. C. A. Kofoid, of the Department of Zoölogy, for his interest and valuable suggestions regarding this problem, and to Dr. M. E. Simpson and associates, of the Department of Anatomy, for assistance in the difficult techniques involved, and for criticism of the hematological investigations.

MATERIALS

The recently discovered California strain of *Trypanosoma cruzi* Chagas from laboratory-infected cone-nose bugs (*Triatoma protracta* Uhler) was used for inoculation of animals. Wood (1934b), while working out the life cycle of the organism, discovered that certain mammals, namely, several species of white-footed mice (*Peromyscus*), were especially susceptible to the infection. Because of the docility of the Southern Parasitic Mouse (*Peromyscus californicus insignis* Rhoads) and its adaptability to laboratory conditions, the author used this animal for experimentation. Specimens were obtained from Los Angeles and San Diego counties in California, and others were raised in the laboratory from this stock.

METHODS

In the study of the blood and tissues, only adult, sexually mature male mice were used. All animals were weighed before the experiments were begun. The average weight was 30 (25–36) gm. for control mice, and 42 (38–47) gm. for experimental mice. The feces of all mice were examined for intestinal worms. No evidences of worm infection were found, although some animals showed

[389]

amoebae and *Trichomonas*. One normal animal was found to be parasitized near the anus by a *Cuterebra* larva after determinations were begun. This probably accounted for a high white-cell count on the fifth day, at which time the larva was removed, with seemingly no ill effects to the mouse. Each mouse was inoculated intraperitoneally with a 0.3 cc. suspension of infective intestinal contents of one adult *Triatoma protracta* in sodium citrate solution (1 gm. of sodium chloride and 1 gm. of sodium citrate in 200 cc. of double-distilled water). No experimentally inoculated mice died from the infection. All control mice were inoculated intraperitoneally with 0.3 cc. of sodium citrate solution.

Because of the reported stimulation of erythropoiesis in mice by repeated bleeding (Scarborough, 1930), sufficient time, namely, six days, was allowed between samplings to avoid interference with the normal process. The total period of sampling was thirty-six days. In order to cover every day of the infection, counts were made on two mice (one infected and one control) on the 1st, 7th, 13th, 19th, 25th, and 31st day after inoculation, on two others on the 2d, 8th, 14th, 20th, 26th, and 32d day, and so forth, until six sets were completed. In this manner the effects of experimental hemorrhage were avoided, and the site of sampling had time to heal before the next samples were taken. Blood was taken from the veins of the ears, which are large and almost hairless in these mice, the vessel being cut transversely with the sharp corner of a razor blade.

Red- and white-cell counts were made according to common practice (Stitt, 1927) with a certified Bausch and Lomb hemocytometer. Hemoglobin estimations were made with a Hellige normal hemometer. All readings were taken after one-half hour to insure complete change of the hemoglobin to acid hematin. Reticulocyte counts were made according to Pappenheim's (1907) method. The percentage of reticulocytes for one thousand red cells was noted. Differential leucocyte counts were made upon smears stained with May-Giemsa. For nearly every animal two hundred white blood cells per smear were counted in such a way that all four sides of the smear were sampled. The average number is here given, followed in parentheses by the range for each cell type.

The procedure for making the determinations was as follows. The animal was placed in a cylinder of $\frac{5}{16}$-inch square galvanized wire-cloth netting (20 gauge), one end of which was pointed and soldered together. The mouse was held in place by inserting two small sticks behind it through the netting. This arrangement allowed the animal to be in a normal resting position, with the ears protruding through the netting. The *right* ear was cleaned with 95 per cent alcohol and then gently wiped dry with a piece of sterile cotton. One or two veins, depending upon the rapidity of bleeding, were slit transversely with a razor and the blood taken into the hemometer pipette and immediately diluted. Then, one or two drops of blood from the ear were diluted with Ringer's solution for the reticulocyte count. The *left* ear was cleaned and wiped and one vein slit and the sample taken in the red pipette to the 0.1 mark only. The dilution was made with Hayem's solution. The cut was then wiped clean and a sample taken in the white pipette to the 0.1 mark and diluted with 1 per cent acetic acid in distilled water. The cut was again wiped clean and the next one or two drops were used for smears.

Smears were tested for oxydase ferment by the following method. Air-dried films were treated with a benzidine solution (100 mg. benzidine, 20 cc. methyl alcohol, 5 cc. distilled water, 1 drop of hydrogen peroxide) which after 30 seconds was diluted one-half with a 0.1 per cent aqueous copper-sulphate solution, and this allowed to act for 2 minutes. The slides were washed in distilled water and then stained with Giemsa's blood stain for 10 minutes, washed in distilled water, and dried. After being thoroughly dried, they were mounted in Grübler's euparal-green or neutral Canada balsam. Smears fixed by Knoll's (1932) method and treated with benzidine solution alone gave the best results.

Normal blood was studied with neutral red and Janus green in separate solutions as well as mixtures. Only fresh preparations were used, the preparations being immediately discarded on evidence of degeneration. Smears of the blood and impression smears of the spleen and of the bone marrow stained with May-Giemsa, Jenner-Giemsa, and Pappenheim's panchrome were also studied. Sections of the spleen, sternum, and lymph nodes were prepared after infiltration and embedding in mixtures of nitrocellulose and ether-alcohol by the method of Dr. Alexis Koneff, of the Department of Anatomy, University of California. All sections of the spleen were sagittal or parasagittal, and were mounted on slides and the embedding mixture removed after Maximow's (1909) method. Some sections of all tissues were stained in Delafield's hematoxylin and eosin. Spleen sections were stained with Pappenheim's (1911) panchrome, Mallory-azan, silver-gold-Harris's hematoxylin-Van Giesen, Harris's hematoxylin and Van Giesen, and May-Grünwald-Giemsa (Petri, 1930). Sections of sternum were stained with the three combinations last mentioned.

MORPHOLOGY OF THE NORMAL BLOOD

The *red blood corpuscles* (pl. 20, fig. 2) are typically small biconcave disks. The average number per cubic millimeter for twelve mice was 10,600,000 (9,600,000–12,910,000). The average diameter of one hundred corpuscles chosen at random from air-dried smears was 5.3μ, with a range of 4.2–6.9μ. Throughout the blood of normal animals Howell-Jolly bodies were seen occasionally in the red corpuscles, especially while differential leucocyte counts were being made, but the actual rate per thousand red corpuscles was very small, since only one or two were found on a few slides. The average percentage of reticulocytes for twelve mice was 2.5, and of polychromatic corpuscles 1.0.

The differentiation of leucocyte types follows the work of Petri (1933, 1934) for the blood of white mice. The terminology of Pappenheim and Hirschfeld (1920) has been used in descriptions of cell structure. In contrast to the blood of white mice, the nuclei of all granular leucocytes in the blood of *Peromyscus* are typically ring-shaped (pl. 20, figs. 1, 3–12). This ringlike appearance is often masked by the overlapping of adjacent parts, so that at times, with deeply stained cells, a typical horseshoe-shaped nucleus may appear. Close inspection, however, reveals their ring character. The width of the ring in the neutrophils is such that it allows for some flexibility and twisting, in contrast to the nuclei of eosinophils and basophils. In a few cells, a nucleus was found with no connecting threads between the lobes. However, it is doubtful whether cells with this type of nucleus are normal constituents of the blood; they may be artifacts caused by smearing or fixation.

The average number of leucocytes per cubic millimeter for twelve mice was 10,100 (3,750–16,750). Noticeable in the differential leucocyte counts of normal mice is the large variation in numbers of type *a* neutrophils, type *a* eosinophils, and medium and small lymphocytes.

The *neutrophil leucocytes* are divided into three types: multilobulated, segmented, and unsegmented. The multilobulated form (pl. 20, fig. 5) is rare, constituting 0.29 (0.0–1.0) per cent of the white cells. The nucleus of this type is distinctly pinched off into three to five definite lobules connected by narrow chromatin strands. The contour of the lobules is smooth. The segmented type (pl. 20, figs. 6, 7) is most numerous. There are two rather distinct stages of the segmented type, which are designated as *a* and *b*. Type *a* (pl. 20, fig. 6) is applied to a nucleus which is distinctly segmented in several places, in contrast to type *b* (pl. 20, fig. 7), which shows only one distinct segmentation. Segmentation refers to the constriction of distinct masses of the nucleus from one another, leaving only narrow connections. This differs from the lobulated condition only in the width of the connecting part between separate segments. Here it is usually a definite band, in contrast to the threadlike connections between the lobules of the multilobulated type. Thus, type *a* refers to a segmented and lobulated arrangement of the nuclear mass, whereas type *b* refers to a single segmentation without distinct lobulation. The contour of the nucleus of type *a* is irregular and uneven, whereas that of type *b* tends to be smoother. Type *a* constitutes 26.16 (12.5–46.5) per cent, whereas type *b* represents only 0.70 (0.0–1.5) per cent. The unsegmented type (pl. 20, fig. 8) has a simple, round, even-contoured, ringlike nucleus with a definite aperture. It is rarely found in the circulating blood, and then not in all animals.

The nucleus of all neutrophils is fundamentally the same in structure. The chromatin (basichromatin) is distinctly clumped or banded, separated within the lobes and between the lobes by narrow parachromatin (oxychromatin) spaces. Sometimes the clumps are broken up, but the chromatic parts retain a homogeneous deep-staining capacity. The chromatin masses of the multilobular type (pl. 20, fig. 5) tend to be darker, more homogeneous, and more compact, suggestive of older cells and the beginning of nuclear degeneration. The nuclei of the segmented types (pl. 20, figs. 6, 7) show less dense chromatin masses separated by distinct spaces. The unsegmented type (pl. 20, fig. 8) shows the youngest type of nucleus, for the chromatin appears in definite narrow strands separated by narrow parachromatin spaces.

The cytoplasm of the various types of neutrophils varies less than does their nuclear structure. In the older cells, with multilobulated and segmented nuclei, the spongioplasmatic network seems to have disappeared, leaving a distinctly oxyphilic paraplasm. However, this is not always so, since sometimes the cytoplasm has a basophilic appearance. In the unsegmented type, the blue-staining spongioplasm tends to overcast the pink-staining paraplasm, so that the cytoplasm has a definite blue, netted appearance. The average diameter of thirty segmented type *a* neutrophils was 10.8μ, with cells ranging in size from 8.4 to 11.7μ.

The neutrophil granules are less distinct when destaining is prolonged to bring out differentiation of lymphocytes. The granules are small, irregular in size and shape, and are purple-violet to light pink (pseudo eosinophilic). They are best seen in overstained parts of the smear, where they stand out as separate, distinct particles. Not all the granules stain with the same intensity, for some show a definite pinkish cast even in the more heavily stained cells. Most of the cells, except the unsegmented type, have many granules scattered throughout the cytoplasm.

The *eosinophil leucocytes* (pl. 20, figs. 9, 10) are of two types, on the basis of nuclear structure. Here, in contrast to the neutrophils, the nuclei of both types are smooth-contoured, but the nucleus of type *a* (pl. 20, fig. 9) is more regular in shape than the nucleus of type *b* (pl. 20, fig. 10). The width of the chromatin mass in type *a* is greater than that of the segmented neutrophils and, when in the form of a circle, surrounds a large aperture. The nucleus of type *a* may be circular, knotted at one end in a figure 8, or folded upon itself in the shape of a horseshoe. The nucleus of type *b* is regular in outline, not twisted, but in simple circular form, enclosing a much smaller aperture. Type *a* constitutes 6.62 (1.5–17.0) per cent of the white cells, whereas type *b* constitutes 0.37 (0.0–2.0) per cent.

The nucleus of eosinophils of type *a* (pl. 20, fig. 9) shows fine and coarse strands or clumps of chromatin scattered throughout the nucleus and separated by narrow parachromatin spaces. The chromatin of type *b* (pl. 20, fig. 10) is more homogeneous in appearance, being distributed throughout the nucleus in broader bands and separated by parachromatin spaces of varying widths.

The cytoplasm of the eosinophils is basophilic where visible among the granules. There is no evidence of a netlike meshwork of spongioplasm. The average diameter of thirty type *a* eosinophils was 10.6μ, with cells ranging in size from 9.3 to 11.7μ.

The eosinophil granules are large, round, highly refractile bodies of uniform size and shape scattered throughout the cytoplasm and in most cells they fill it completely. They vary in color from a distinct dark brownish orange to orange-pink.

The *basophil leucocytes* (pl. 20, figs. 11, 12) of the circulating blood represent two types on the basis of nuclear structure. The nuclei of both are regular in outline, like those of the eosinophils. The nucleus of type *a* (pl. 20, fig. 11) appears either in circular form or in the shape of a figure 8, but is not as plastic as that of the eosinophils or neutrophils, possibly because of its greater width. The nucleus of type *b* (pl. 20, fig. 12) has a much smaller aperture and is always of simple circular form. Sometimes clumps of granules obscure the hole in the nucleus. Type *a* is represented by 2.75 (0.5–11.5) per cent, whereas type *b* constitutes 0.50 (0.0–2.0) per cent.

The nucleus of basophils shows broad, homogeneous chromatin masses separated by narrow parachromatin spaces. Some of the older cells of type *a* show more parachromatin, tending to break up the homogeneous aspect of the nucleus.

The cytoplasm of the basophil leucocyte is bluish (basophilic) where visible, although in some cells there may be a pinkish cast. The average diameter of thirty type *a* basophils was 11.6μ, with cells ranging in size from 9.6 to 13.8μ.

The basophil granules are large, uniform-sized, dark-purple-staining, ovoidal bodies which are closely crowded together and generally fill the cytoplasm completely.

The *small lymphocytes* (pl. 20, fig. 17) have a simple round, or slightly indented, eccentric nucleus which stains very deeply because of the broad, homogeneous, interconnecting chromatin masses. The parachromatin spaces are limited to narrow areas between the chromatin masses. They constitute 43.66 (18.0–61.0) per cent of the total white cells.

The cytoplasm of the small lymphocytes is limited to a very narrow zone completely encircling the nucleus. Generally, the cytoplasm is visible on one side only, and is deeply basophilic, with a distinct spongioplasmatic network. The tint varies from dark to light blue, and the outermost rim is usually darkest, with a lighter area immediately surrounding the nucleus or at its indentation. Where the cytoplasm is limited to one side of the cell, the characteristic perinuclear halo is also visible only on that side. The paraplasm is blue to gray-blue. The average diameter of thirty small lymphocytes was 7.8μ.

The *medium-sized lymphocytes* (pl. 20, fig. 19) often show the typical nuclear structure of small lymphocytes. Sometimes the nucleus of these cells shows more definite chromatin clumps or masses separated by greater parachromatin spaces. Medium-sized lymphocytes constitute 9.41 (3.5–23.5) per cent of the total white cells.

The cytoplasm of the medium-sized lymphocytes is a broader zone which encircles the nucleus completely. Occasionally the nucleus is decidedly eccentric, but usually some cytoplasm is visible all around it. The cytoplasm of these lymphocytes stains lighter blue than that of the small lymphocyte, tending to show a broader perinuclear halo. The average diameter of thirty medium-sized lymphocytes was 9.3μ.

The azure granules of the small and medium-sized lymphocytes are variable in size and scattered throughout the cytoplasm. They stain pale violet to pink. The larger cells usually show more granules than the smaller cells. In some cells there appear definite groups of granules besides other large homogeneous granules (pl. 20, fig. 18). The appearance of these bodies suggests either ingested platelets, or extranuclear chromatin masses, or Kurloff bodies, but their exact nature is unknown. These bodies were found but sparsely in the lymphocytes and mononuclears of the blood of both normal and infected mice.

The *large lymphocytes* (pl. 20, fig. 16) show noticeable structural variation. Some have simple, indented, or kidney-shaped nuclei which show very distinct broad chromatin clumps and masses. The parachromatin spaces are narrow or slightly broader areas between the chromatin masses. These large lymphocytes are easily recognized because of the close similarity of their nuclear structure to that of the small and medium-sized lymphocytes. Rarely, cells with a hole in the nucleus were found (myelocytes ?). There are other large lymphocytes in which the chromatin is separated into more or less distinct clumps or masses with wider parachromatin spaces. In some cells there are only one or two distinct homogeneous chromatin masses in the middle or at one side of the nucleus, the rest of the nucleus showing a definite meshwork of narrow chromatin strands and narrow parachromatin spaces. These cells seem to be borderline examples between the large lymphocytes and the mononuclears and on the basis of nuclear structure alone are difficult to distinguish. The large lymphocytes make up 5.08 (2.5–9.0) per cent of the total white cells.

The cytoplasm of the large lymphocytes shows a broad protoplasmic zone exhibiting various degrees of basophilia. A definite perinuclear halo is usually visible. The dark blue spongioplasm is most distinct toward the periphery of the cell, whereas the bluish gray paraplasm is most distinct next to the nucleus or in the region of the nuclear indentation. In some cells, however, the cytoplasm is limited to a narrow zone around a very large nucleus. The presence of a distinct perinuclear halo within a broad, light-staining cytoplasm, plus the characteristic nuclear features, makes accurate classification possible. The average diameter of thirty large lymphocytes was 10.8μ. The range in size of all forms of lymphocytes was from 6.3 to 13.8μ.

The azure granules of the large lymphocytes are few to many and are irregularly scattered throughout the cytoplasm. In some cells there are large azurophilic granules about one-half the size of basophil granules.

The *mononuclear cells* (pl. 20, figs. 13, 14) are among the largest leucocytes of the blood. They constitute 4.66 (1.0–10.5) per cent of the white cells. The largest cell measured 13.8μ, the same as the largest lymphocyte. The nucleus is simple, indented, kidney-shaped, horseshoe-shaped, or sometimes coarsely lobular. The chromatin is distributed throughout the nucleus in fine strands and clumps which are separated by equally extensive areas of parachromatin. This results in a netted or meshlike homogeneous appearance of the nucleus, in contrast to the clumped chromatin masses seen in the nuclei of lymphocytes. In some mononuclears there may be one or two more extensive chromatin masses, with the rest of the nucleus showing the typical meshwork of chromatin and parachromatin. The mononuclears lack the distinct halo and structural uniformity of the cytoplasm of the large lymphocytes. In some cells the edges of the nucleus tend to be composed of an interrupted narrow band of homogeneous-appearing chromatin strips.

The cytoplasm of the mononuclears shows a distinct, darkly stained, bluish, spongioplasmatic network with a lighter-staining, often pinkish or gray, paraplasm. The netted and vacuolated aspect gives as distinctive an appearance to the cytoplasm as does the meshwork of chromatin and parachromatin to the nucleus. Most mononuclears show no evidence of a lighter area immediately surrounding the nucleus. Some show a perinuclear halo much like that of the lymphocytes. Sometimes there are several large vacuoles in the cytoplasm. The average diameter of thirty mononuclears was 11.7μ, ranging from 10.2 to 13.8μ.

The azure granules of the mononuclears are numerous, faintly visible, and irregularly scattered throughout the cytoplasm. Sometimes there are a few larger azurophilic granules here, as in the large lymphocytes.

The *blood platelets* (pl. 20, fig. 2) are small, usually rounded, masses of protoplasm containing a group of small chromatin-like granules. These distinctly outlined basophilic, protoplasmic masses are irregular in size, shape, and number of the chromatin-like granules within the protoplasm, and range in diameter from 1 to 3μ.

The oxydase reaction was positive in all types of neutrophil and eosinophil leucocytes (pl. 20, figs. 1, 3, 4), and negative in all types of basophil leucocytes, lymphocytes, and mononuclears. The granules of the neutrophil leucocytes after fixation by Knoll's (1932) method gave a pronounced positive reaction (pl. 20, fig. 1). The specific granules appear as irregularly shaped, yellowish green masses which tend to be spherical in form. The cytoplasm of some cells is almost completely filled with these granules. Other cells of the same type may show few or many granules, but all types of cells show at least a few granules in their cytoplasm. There seemed to be fewer oxydase granules per cell in slides treated without the fixative. Some granules seemed to give a stronger reaction than others, so that in some cells all grades of color intensity were observed. With copper sulphate the granules are greenish blue after Knoll's fixative, but without the fixative they have a distinct bluish tint. Knoll found that the oxydase reaction in neutrophils of rodents (*Mus musculus* and others) was exceedingly variable with respect to shape and number of granules. Most rodents showed the reaction, but the guinea pig and rabbit showed oxydase-negative neutrophils. The reaction was always positive in eosinophils and negative for basophils and lymphocytes. Most of the monocytes from the different species of animals gave no reaction at all, whereas in some forms, such as the monotremes, there was a positive reaction, although even there it was by no means so definite as that observed in the eosinophils and neutrophils.

The oxydase reaction of eosinophil leucocytes (pl. 20, fig. 3) was more decidedly positive than that of the neutrophils. Whether or not a fixative was used, the eosinophils always exhibited distinct, rounded, highly refractile, yellowish brown to greenish granules which usually filled the cytoplasm completely. With copper sulphate these granules did not react, thus tending to retain the tint from the benzidine treatment only.

Supravital staining differentiates the leucocytes chiefly by the appearance of the specific granules, but also by the distribution of the mitochondria and the appearance of the segregation apparatus. The neutrophils show distinct, small, nonrefractile granules. The eosinophil granules are large and refractile, and the basophil granules are largest of all and nonrefractile. The lymphocytes show appreciable diversity of structure and type. The forms seen here lend support to the finding in stained smears of many different types of lymphocytes. The mononuclears are differentiated from the others by the large, often indented nucleus, the distinct group of reddish brown granules at the indentation of the nucleus, and the numerous mitochondrial granules and rodlets scattered throughout the cytoplasm or more uniformly grouped around the mass of neutral red-staining granules.

MORPHOLOGY OF BLOOD INFECTED WITH
TRYPANOSOMA CRUZI

Recorded data show no differences between normal and infected animals with respect to the number of red and of white corpuscles, hemoglobin, reticulocytes, and polychromasia. There were some changes in the differential leucocyte counts, as is noted below. From the incomplete survey of the normal blood no final comparison can be made of the size and shape of the red corpuscles in different animals, and in the same animal at different times. However, one animal which had five times the usual dosage of infective material, having been inoculated daily for five consecutive days from a total of five bugs, showed increased polychromasia. There were 4.0 per cent of these cells on the 17th day following the first inoculation, and 4.7 per cent on the 20th day, in contrast to 0.5 per cent and 0.7 per cent, respectively, for the controls, and 1.2 per cent and 1.6 per cent, respectively, for the experimental mice with a single inoculation.

The increase in the number of large lymphocytes (pl. 20, fig. 15) in later stages of the infection was the most constant and striking feature in the microscopic picture of the circulating leucocytes. The blood of experimental mice showed an increase of 5.71 (0.0–15.5) per cent per day from the 14th to the 36th day (except the 25th and 31st days, each minus 1.5 per cent) of the infection. Although this indicates only a small change, the difference is readily noted in counting. The large lymphocytes, as a whole, are more uniform not only in size but also in structure, those from infected animals having well-defined, broad interconnecting chromatin bands with narrow parachromatin spaces. The zone of cytoplasm is broad and lightly basophilic, with large intracytoplasmic granules in some cells. The irregularity of the nucleus in some of these cells and its dense homogeneous appearance suggest the beginning of karyolysis, and some of these larger granules may be a product of this action. Besides these more numerous, typical, large lymphocytes there appear other lymphocytes which show more widely separated, definite chromatin clumps characteristic of younger cells of the lymphocytic series.

The eosinophils (type *a*) showed an average numerical decrease of 5.81 (0.5–14.67) per cent per day from the 26th to 36th day after inoculation, except the 34th day (+2.5 per cent). This is substantiated by the increased number of these cells in the spleen. Evidently, their response is enlisted at the sites of activity in resistance to the infection.

The neutrophils showed a tendency toward greater irregularity in structure and lobulation of the nucleus in some infected animals. Most cells of normal blood showed three to five lobules, whereas many in infected animals showed six to eight.

The platelets probably decreased in number during the first part of the infection, since the ears of infected mice bled more freely, suggesting interference with the clotting mechanism. No counts were made, but the appearance of more megakaryocytes in the spleen and bone marrow suggests that such an effect was present.

MORPHOLOGY OF THE NORMAL SPLEEN

The normal spleens were taken from three mice the weights of which were 28, 34 (pl. 21, figs. 20, 23; pl. 22, figs. 24, 26), and 47 gm., respectively. The histology of the normal spleen of the Southern Parasitic Mouse is much like that of man, except that in the mouse the follicles of the white pulp are larger and more extensive in relation to the size of the spleen. Its structure is similar to that of the spleen in the white mouse (Hoyer, 1894; Downey and Weidenreich, 1912; Jaffé, 1921, 1931; Jolly, 1923; Klienenberger and Carl, 1927; Hartmann, 1930; Maximow and Bloom, 1931), the rabbit (Hoyer, 1894; Dominici, 1900a, 1901; Jaffé, 1931), and the rat (Hu, 1931; Jaffé, 1931). In comparison with the extent of the spleen in parasagittal section, the follicles in *Peromyscus*, which generally stand out sharply from the surrounding red pulp, are approximately one-fourth the width of the organ, rarely larger. Since the masses of lymphocytes which constitute the follicles are distributed along the arterial channels, their course through the spleen is variable.

Most follicles show definite secondary nodules or the beginnings of such nodules (pl. 21, fig. 20; pl. 22, fig. 24). These secondary nodules consist of medium and large lymphocytes and intermediate forms with lymphoblasts scattered throughout, as well as phagocytes and fixed reticular cells. However, these germinal centers are always enclosed within masses of smaller lymphocytes of the primary nodules, even though there are only a few cell layers between the edge of the secondary nodule and the reticular membrane inside the marginal zone (Downey and Weidenreich, 1912). Sometimes the follicles show only the dense masses of small lymphocytes with scattered larger lymphocytes, lymphoblasts, and reticular cells characteristic of the primary nodules. Outside the reticular membrane around the follicle is the narrow marginal zone composed mostly of medium-sized and large lymphocytes and infiltrated with red blood corpuscles, small lymphocytes, and large and medium-sized lymphoblasts from the red pulp. In some places the marginal zone is very narrow and the venous sinuses of the red pulp lie close to the reticular membrane of the follicle (Hartmann, 1930). However, no venous sinuses were found in the marginal zone.

The red pulp constitutes relatively wide areas or zones between the follicles (pl. 21, fig. 20). The spaces between the sinuses in the red pulp are heavily infiltrated with lymphocytes, lymphoblasts, eosinophil myelocytes, eosinophil and neutrophil leucocytes, free reticular cells (macrophages), erythroblasts, a few plasma cells, and a few megakaryocytes. The nuclei of the megakaryocytes appear either as mononuclear or multilobulated, the latter form being the predominant type. The general appearance of the red pulp, however, is that of a loose meshwork with scattered free cells in and among the venous sinuses, which are well filled with red corpuscles, and here and there small groups of polychromatophylic erythroblasts (pl. 21, fig. 23). The writer's findings on the free cellular constituents of the red pulp of the spleen of *Peromyscus* agree in general with the findings for the spleen of the white mouse by Downey and Weidenreich (1912), Jaffé (1921, 1931), Jolly (1923),

Klienenberger and Carl (1927), Hartmann (1930), and Maximow and Bloom (1931). Jolly (1923) says the megakaryocytes are numerous, whereas Maximow and Bloom (1931) say they occur in small numbers. Klienenberger and Carl (1927) found them sometimes numerous, sometimes scanty. Jaffé (1931) found that the distribution of all pulp cells was very irregular, whereas Hartmann (1930) found that megakaryocytes accumulate in the regions of the capsule and trabeculae. The three normal spleens of *Peromyscus* all showed megakaryocytes widely scattered in small numbers throughout the organ but tending to accumulate near the capsule and trabeculae. Hartmann (1930) states that mast cells are generally found in the spleen of white mice, but these were not noted inside the spleen of *Peromyscus*. Only small amounts of pigment were found here in the pulp, in agreement with the findings of Hartmann (1930) for white mice.

The distribution of the connective tissue and reticular framework of the organ is similar to that of the human spleen. The capsule and trabeculae have few smooth muscle cells as in the spleen of white mice (Hoyer, 1894; Hartmann, 1930). The reticulum of the spleen of *Peromyscus* is sharply defined after silver-gold treatment as distinct, coarse, interconnecting, rounded fibrils, which is in agreement with the findings of Jolly (1923) for white mice. Hoyer (1894) reported the presence of a fine, delicate reticulum in the spleen of white mice, but admitted difficulties with technique. The size of the spleen and degree of development of the follicles vary with the age of the animal. The older (heavier) mice show more secondary nodules in the follicles, whereas the younger mice show fewer secondary and mostly primary nodules.

CHANGES IN THE TISSUES WITH INFECTION

SPLEEN

Five infected mice weighing 20, 33, 41, 43, and 50 gm., respectively, were used in studies of the changes caused in the spleen by infection. No differences were noted in the amount or distribution of connective tissue or reticulum in normal and infected animals. The general reaction shown in varying degrees by all infected spleens was toward increased cellular proliferation (pl. 21, figs. 21, 22; pl. 22, fig. 25), especially in the germinal centers of the follicles and to some degree in the free cells of the red pulp. Some spleens were enlarged as much as twice the normal, whereas others showed no increase in size. Enlargement of the spleen is a common accompaniment of infection with *Trypanosoma cruzi*, as pointed out by Castellani and Chalmers (1919), Crowell (1923), Mazza (1926*b*), Niño (1929), and DeCoursey (1935).

The follicles tended definitely to increase in size, becoming three to five times larger than normal. The entire aspect of the follicle was changed, owing to the hyperplasia of the cells of the secondary nodules, as evidenced by increased numbers of division figures in all stages of mitosis and the partial to nearly complete obliteration of the compact small lymphocyte masses of the primary nodules (pl. 22, fig. 25). The cells of the secondary nodules are chiefly large and medium-sized lymphocytes and lymphoblasts, with fixed and free reticular cells (macrophages) scattered throughout. There was a marked increase in the number of free reticular cells the protoplasm of which was crowded with ingested cellular remains in various stages of degeneration. In extreme cases the character of the follicle was entirely changed, owing to the obliteration of the primary nodules by the hyperplasia of the cells in the secondary nodules. Mitotic figures were then common throughout the follicles. More often, at one side or another, or almost completely enclosing the secondary nodule, was a narrow zone of small lymphocytes of the primary nodule, just inside the reticular membrane of the follicle. The marginal zone tended to broaden in some instances and become more completely infiltrated with cells of the red pulp, though retaining its homogeneous-appearing zonation surrounding the follicle, a result of the preponderance of medium-sized and large lymphocytes.

The red pulp, in extreme examples, showed under low magnification a decidedly blotchy appearance (pl. 21, fig. 21), owing to the presence of compact clumps of polychromatophylic erythroblasts, small lymphocytes, plasma cells, and eosinophils in the tissue spaces between the congested venous sinuses. The blotchiness was emphasized chiefly by the very dense nuclear structure of the many scattered groups of erythroblasts. The groups of small lymphocytes and plasma cells were more numerous here than in normal spleens and were scattered throughout the red pulp of the organ, suggesting active transformation of plasma cells from small lymphocytes, as shown by Bloom (1928) and Hu and Ch'in (1933). Occasional mitotic figures among eosinophil myelocytes, also indicative of myeloid metaplasia, were found throughout the red pulp, but chiefly along the trabeculae and in the subcapsular zones. Mitotic figures of lymphoblasts were also found in scattered clumps of lymphocytes in the red pulp. The lymphoblasts of the red pulp were the same in structure as those found in the germinal centers of the follicles. The eosinophils accumulated in areas where there were many macrophages active in phagocytosis. There were increased numbers of neutrophils, and free reticular cells and eosinophils were seen migrating through the lining of the sinusoids. In some spleens there was an increase in the number of megakaryocytes, so that in some parts of the red pulp six to eight could be seen in a single field with a magnification of 2700 diameters. No trypanosomes or leishmania bodies were found in the spleens. Histologically, this general reaction of the spleen of *Peromyscus* accords almost exactly with the findings reported by Crowell (1923) and DeCoursey (1935) for the spleens of human infants who died of Chagas' disease.

The specific reactions of the spleens of each of the five mice were so different as to warrant individual description. In the 50-gram mouse, which received one inoculation and was killed on the 23d day, the spleen showed a pronounced reaction (pl. 21, fig. 22). The organ was about twice the normal size. The follicles were three or four times as large as normal, and the cellular changes in the follicles were as described above for the more acute reaction. The red pulp showed the largest number of megakaryocytes of any infected spleen, along with many large lymphocytes and small accumulations of erythroblasts. Small numbers of plasma cells were scattered throughout the red pulp.

The 43-gram mouse, which weighed 48 gm. just before its death, was given one inoculation and was killed 276 days (approximately nine months) later. The spleen was only slightly larger than normal, but showed larger germinal centers. The red pulp showed a heavier infiltration of free cells, with small groups of eosinophils as well as single eosinophils scattered along the trabeculae and through the subcapsular zones. There were also a few groups of erythroblasts scattered in the pulp.

The 41-gram mouse received one inoculation and was killed 24 days later. The spleen showed no increase in size and less change than that observed in any other animal. The follicles did not differ from the normal, but the red pulp, especially around some follicles, showed greater numbers of lymphocytes. Scattered throughout the red pulp were more erythroblasts and plasma cells than normal.

The 33-gram mouse had been given five inoculations in all, namely, one inoculation daily for five successive days, using one bug each time, and was killed on the 21st day following the first inoculation. The spleen was about twice normal size and the follicles were from three to five times as large as normal. The obliteration of primary nodules was more complete here than in any other mouse (pl. 21, fig. 21; pl. 22, figs. 25, 27). The red pulp showed the most noticeable blotching, from the presence of many compact accumulations of polychromatophylic erythroblasts, small lymphocytes, and plasma cells.

The 20-gram mouse, which was about two-thirds grown and but recently weaned, had been given a daily inoculation for five successive days, each inoculation being the gut content of two bugs. This mouse was killed on the 27th day after the first inoculation. The spleen was about normal in size. The follicles were enlarged, but not so much so as in either the 50- or the 41-gram mouse. They showed distinct secondary nodules. The primary nodules formed a narrow zone surrounding the germinal centers and were one or two cell layers thick in only a few places between the secondary nodules and the reticular membrane of the follicle. The red pulp showed accumulation of groups of free pulp cells, thus giving it a blotchier appearance than normal.

Bone Marrow

The work of Petri (1934) on white mice has been followed for identification of bone-marrow cells. Counts were made on sections of sternal marrow of 1000 free cells, exclusive of nonnucleated red blood corpuscles, to determine the proportion of megakaryocytes in the different animals. There were 5 per 1000 in the 34-gram normal mouse, 10 per 1000 in the 50-gram infected mouse, 6 per 1000 in the 41-gram infected mouse, and 13 per 1000 in the 33-gram infected mouse. Comparative counts of 500 cells from femur impression and streaked smears in a 41- and a 33-gram infected mouse showed no significant changes from counts on a 36-gram normal mouse.

Lymph Nodes

In a single lumbar lymph node approximately 0.5 mm. in diameter, from the 47-gram normal mouse, there were five or six follicles scattered about the periphery of the gland just under the cortex. The dense masses of small lymphocytes which composed the periphery of the follicle stood out from the surrounding, more loosely constructed medullary tissue. Several follicles showed well-developed germinal centers composed chiefly of medium-sized and large lymphocytes with fixed and free reticular cells scattered throughout. The interfollicular tissue, composed mostly of small lymphocytes, with scattered medium-sized lymphocytes, plasma cells, macrophages, and occasional eosinophils, completely fills the rest of the gland with the exception of some areas in the medulla, where the lymphatic vessels anastomose before leaving the gland. The interfollicular spaces are here almost filled with reticular and lymphoid cells, as in the mesenteric lymph glands of white mice (Downey and Weidenreich, 1912). Inside the connective tissue of the capsule, as well as in the sinuses just under the capsule, were isolated mast cells or groups of mast cells. A few were found in the medullary cords near the center of the gland. This agrees essentially with the findings of Downey and Weidenreich (1912) for the mesenteric lymph glands of white mice, but they emphasize that there is great structural variability in individual lymph glands, even from the same animal.

In the 41- and in the 50-gram mouse, the inguinal lymph nodes were enlarged, and in the latter mouse the bronchial lymph nodes were also enlarged. In the 20-gram mouse there were two enlarged lumbar lymph nodes each measuring about 3 mm. in length. These nodes showed thirteen to fifteen active germinal centers scattered throughout the cortex and medulla of the glands. The primary nodules were obliterated in most of the follicles by the larger germinal centers composed of numerous mitotic figures scattered among the medium-sized and large lymphocytes, and numerous macrophages which were actively phagocytic. Where the primary nodules persisted, it was difficult to tell where the follicle ended and the interfollicular tissue began. The interfollicular tissue, composed chiefly of small and medium-sized lymphocytes, a few eosinophils, and plasma cells, completely filled the spaces between the follicles, except for scattered blood vessels and reticular cells. Mast cells, either singly or in groups, were found in the connective tissue of the capsule and trabeculae. Some isolated mast cells were found in the central parts of the glands in the sinuses and in the tissue between the sinuses. The changes observed here were similar to those observed by Crowell (1923) in the lymph nodes of an eight-month-old female mulatto infected with *T. cruzi*. He found that there were marked congestion, lymphoid hyperplasia, and active phagocytosis in the cervical, axillary, and inguinocrural nodes.

DISCUSSION

The normal blood picture of white mice has been thoroughly studied by De Kock (1931) and Petri (1933, 1934). No attempts were made by De Kock to subdivide the various cell types beyond lymphocytes, monocytes, neutrophils, eosinophils, and basophils, since he maintains that only these forms are recognizable by the three methods of tissue culture, supravital preparation, and May-Grünwald-Giemsa staining. Petri recognizes among the neutrophils, proleucocytes, ring forms, and complicated nuclear forms. The writer's unsegmented neutrophils correspond to Petri's (pl. 1, figs. 1, 2, 5) proleucocytes. The ring forms of Petri (pl. 1, figs. 6 to 13), however, include the segmented and multilobulated forms of the blood of *Peromyscus*. The neutrophils of *Peromyscus* are less variable in structure than those of white mice. There are no neutrophils in this white-footed mouse comparable to Petri's complicated nuclear forms. The type *a* and type *b* eosinophils of white mice correspond to type *a* and type *b* eosinophils of the blood of *Peromyscus*. The basophil leucocytes here, in contrast to those of white mice, possess definite ring-shaped nuclei like the other granulocytes and have been grouped into types *a* and *b* like the eosinophils. Petri's differentiation of lymphocytes is essentially the same as used here. He characterizes the mononuclears as being of the same size as the human monocyte, yet morphologically they are more like the lymphocyte type, especially with respect to their protoplasm, and so he calls them "large mononuclear cells." The mononuclears of the blood of *Peromyscus* show less variability of nuclear shape than those of the white mouse. Loewenthal (1933, 1934) described the leucocyte types of the field mouse, *Arvicola arvalis*. His main cell types are essentially the same as those found in *Peromyscus*.

Michels (1931) states that in the blood of mammals polychromatic red corpuscles are as abundant as are the reticulocytes. The counts on the blood of *Peromyscus* do not verify this statement.

Before a discussion is given of the pathological findings, it would be well to compare available information with respect to the relative strengths of different strains of *Trypanosoma cruzi*. The California strain, as shown by Kofoid and Donat (1933a) and Wood (1934a, b), runs a rather mild course in all animals investigated. Only in a few laboratory animals were symptoms of infection noticeable. The trypanosomes first appeared in the blood of albino rats from the sixteenth to the twenty-seventh day after inoculation. No laboratory animals were permanently incapacitated in any way or died from the infection, but white-footed mice (*Peromyscus*) were most susceptible to infection. Zuccarini (1930), using four different South American strains, found that white mice were the most sensitive experimental animals. The incubation periods for the four strains ranged from five to twenty days, yet all strains were fatal to adult mice between thirty and ninety days after inoculation. Niño (1929) found that white mice were most susceptible to the Argentine strain. The incubation period ranged from six to forty-one days, the average being nineteen days. Most of the mice died after two months. Galliard (1929) has shown that mice may become infected and die without the appearance of trypanosomes in their peripheral blood. In all animals studied here, trypanosomes were found in the peripheral blood.

Emmanuel Dias (1934) has shown that *Trypanosoma cruzi* may infect man for as long as twelve years. He has also shown (1932a) that the minimum time for organisms to appear in the peripheral blood of dogs is forty minutes by the subcutaneous route and two hours, forty-five minutes by the peritoneal route when numerous organisms are injected. Rapid passage of trypanosomes into the blood stream was also noted after intramuscular inoculation and intracerebral injection. Galliard (1929, 1930) maintains that in white mice the subcutaneous route of inoculation is preferable to the intraperitoneal, in view of the precocity and intensity of the manifestations that it produces. When Dias inoculated white mice with the intestinal contents of infected *Triatoma,* the initial blood phase, mentioned above, did not occur, because the organisms did not appear in the blood until the eleventh day. In one animal inoculated intraperitoneally with the intestinal contents of an infected *Triatoma protracta* (California strain), the author noted the appearance of trypanosomes in blood smears on the seventh day after inoculation, but in other *Peromyscus* the incubation period was longer.

Changes in the blood picture of Chagas' disease have been reported by Eze-quiel Dias (1912), Mazza (1926*a, b*), Geoghegan (1929), MacRobert (1929), and Niño (1929). Dias' work is the most comprehensive hematological investigation on man. Owing to the high incidence of other parasitic infections in the territory studied, Dias had only nineteen cases limited to *Trypanosoma cruzi* infection alone. He compared findings of different cases with normal counts made by himself on persons free from parasites. His results show no anaemia, decreased hemoglobin and specific gravity, slight leucocytosis in acute cases, pronounced macrolymphocytosis in acute cases and recently infected cases, and generally an eosinophilia and light basophilia in old cases. The blood counts by Mazza (1926*b*) and Geoghegan (1929) on single human cases agree with the findings of Dias. MacRobert (1929) reports a high percentage of lymphocytes in the blood for a case with nervous symptoms.

Niño (1929) reports numerous observations on the blood of white mice and other laboratory animals infected with *Trypanosoma cruzi,* Argentine strain. White mice were most susceptible to infection and most of the infected animals died in about two months. There was an intense anaemia of the regenerative type which manifested itself by changes of chromophilia, appearance of nor-moblasts, and especially by the appearance of large numbers of red corpuscles with Howell-Jolly bodies. There was marked anisocytosis, and in some cases an appreciable poikilocytosis. During the course of the infection there was an initial lymphocytosis lasting from one to fifteen or twenty-five days after inoculation, followed by a polymorphonuclear neutrophil leucocytosis, which persisted or returned to a level approximately the same as for the lymphocytes until the death of the animal. In *T. cruzi* infections in dogs, Mazza's (1926*a*) work showed a lymphocytosis. The author's finding of a lymphocytosis agrees with those of Ezequiel Dias (1912) and Niño (1929). It is interesting that with the California strain the postlymphocytic neutrophil leucocytosis was not evident even up to thirty-six days after infection, whereas in Niño's experiments on white mice a neutrophil leucocytosis was generally evident twenty-five to thirty-five days after infection.

It has been noted that splenic enlargement in white mice, accompanied by myeloid metaplasia, is common in some infections (Jarotzky, 1908; Jolly, 1923; Simonds, 1925; McCoy-Hill, 1930). Definite hyperplasia of different cell elements of the spleen, especially the reticulo-endothelial cells, is a general accompaniment of infectious states. Dominici (1900*b*, 1901, 1921) and Maximow (1927) have noted that eosinophil leucocytes are readily mobilized at sites of such reactions, as has also been found in this investigation.

Enlargement of the spleen has been observed in guinea pigs infected with *Trypanosoma congolense* and *T. gambiense* (Laveran, 1908), in rats infected with *T. lewisi* (Marmorston-Gottesman, Perla, and Vorzimer, 1930), in guinea pigs infected with *T. equiperdum* (Poindexter, 1933), and in hamsters and rats infected with *Leishmania donovani* and *T. brucei*, respectively (Hu and Cash, 1929; Hu, 1931, 1933, 1934; Hu and Ch'in, 1933).

In *Trypanosoma cruzi* infections in white mice, Niño (1929) observed in the spleen of different animals hyperplasia of the connective tissue, thickening of the capsule, intense congestion, inflammation, fibrosis, hyperplasia of the lymphoid tissue, and in some spleens abundant blood pigment. A definite hyperplasia of the lymphoid tissue and marked increase in the cellularity of the interfollicular tissue was observed in some spleens of white-footed mice infected with the California strain.

Various peculiarities in tissues have been noted in infections with *Trypanosoma cruzi*. Souza-Campos (1929) found in infected dogs changes in the nuclei of the reticulo-endothelial cells, which contained numerous parasites. Torres and de Azevedo (1929a, b) found numerous multinucleated giant cells in the myocardium of the armadillo, and in the heart, thyroid, and kidneys of dogs experimentally infected from the armadillo. These giant cells showed numerous leishmaniform bodies of *T. cruzi* in their cytoplasm, which was bordered by a distinct membrane forming a true double-walled cyst. Mazza (1930) found these giant cell cysts in the heart and muscle fibers of the bronchi of the armadillo. Villela and Dias (1934a, b) have reported necrotic ulcers of the bones and joints, external genital organs, mouth, skin (hair follicles, epidermis, and dermis), and digestive mucosa (stomach, intestine) in dogs experimentally infected from the armadillo. No such changes were observed in the hematoplastic tissues of mice infected with the California strain.

Locatelli (1929) observed extensive changes in the megakaryocytes of the bone marrow of guinea pigs infected with *Trypanosoma equiperdum* and *T. brucei*. In animals which died three or four months after inoculation, he found nearly all the nuclei of mature megakaryocytes in pycnosis and there were very few young forms in the marrow. In animals which died a short time after inoculation, numerous mitoses of megakaryocytes were found in all stages of division and there were many young forms in the marrow. The effect of the infection on the bone marrow, according to Locatelli, was a stimulation of the mature megakaryocytes toward degeneration and of the young forms toward maturation. Although some increase of cells was noted in the sternal marrow of *Peromyscus*, there was no evidence of degeneration of the nuclei or mitotic figures of the megakaryocytes.

The most important single cellular response in the spleen of *Peromyscus* to the action of the California strain of *Trypanosoma cruzi* is the active proliferation of cells of the reticulo-endothelial system, as described above. Hu (1931, 1934), Marmorston-Gottesman, Perla, and Vorzimer (1930), and Poindexter (1933) have pointed out that the reticulo-endothelial cells are the chief sites of response in other trypanosomiases. Cash and Hu (1929), Hu and Cash (1929), and Hu (1933) have shown that in hamsters infected with kala azar, the most characteristic change is a reticulo-endothelial hyperplasia, but here the action is evidently both mechanical and toxic, since numerous macrophages are found whose cytoplasm is filled with parasites. Some strains of *T. cruzi*, especially in dogs, seem also to give this type of reaction, as shown by Souza-Campos (1929) and Emmanuel Dias (1932*b*). As Dias points out, there exists in such instances an infection blockade of the reticulo-endothelial system.

SUMMARY

1. The normal blood of the white-footed mouse (*Peromyscus*) includes orthochromatic and polychromatic red corpuscles, neutrophil, eosinophil, and basophil leucocytes, lymphocytes, mononuclears, and platelets.

2. An increased number of large lymphocytes in the peripheral blood from fourteen to thirty-six days after inoculation was produced by experimental infection with *Trypanosoma cruzi*, California strain.

3. The eosinophil leucocytes were decreased in number from twenty-six to thirty-six days after inoculation.

4. The histology of the normal spleen of *Peromyscus* is described.

5. Infected mice showed enlargement of the spleen up to twice normal size.

6. Enlarged bronchial, lumbar, and inguinal lymph nodes were found in infected animals.

7. Hyperplasia of the lymphoblasts and lymphocytes of the follicles in the spleen, resulting in increase in size of the follicles from three to five times normal, was observed in animals killed twenty-one to twenty-seven days after inoculation.

8. Myeloid metaplasia was noted in the spleen of some mice, involving increase of erythroblasts and eosinophil myelocytes.

9. Megakaryocytes were increased in sections of spleen and sternal marrow of infected animals.

10. Hyperplasia of the reticulo-endothelial cells of the spleen was produced in white-footed mice by experimental infection with the California strain of *Trypanosoma cruzi*.

LITERATURE CITED

BLOOM, W.
1928. The relationships between lymphocytes, monocytes, and plasma cells. Fol. Haematol., 37:63–69.

CASH, J. R., and HU, C. H.
1929. The clasmatocyte in experimental kala-azar. Trans. of the F. E. A. T. M., 7th Cong., India, 3:44–61, pls. 1–2.

CASTELLANI, A., and CHALMERS, A. J.
1919. Manual of tropical medicine (London, Baillière, Tindall and Cox), ed. 3, 2436 pp., 16 pls., 909 figs. in text.

CROWELL, B. C.
1923. The acute form of American trypanosomiasis: notes on its pathology, with autopsy report and observations on trypanosomiasis cruzi in animals. Am. Jour. Trop. Med., 3:425–454, 10 figs. in text.

DECOURSEY, E.
1935. The first fatal case of Chagas' disease observed on the Isthmus of Panama. Am. Jour. Trop. Med., 15:33–40, 3 figs. in text.

DE KOCK, G. v. D. W.
1931. Studies on the blood of mice. 17th Rept. Dir. Vet. Serv. and An. Ind., Union of South Africa, August, 1931, pp. 573–596.

DIAS, EZEQUIEL
1912. Die Krankheit Carlos Chagas. Haematologische Studien. Mem. Inst. Oswaldo Cruz, 4:34–61.

DIAS, EMMANUEL
1932a. Le *Trypanosoma cruzi* pendant les premières phases de l'infection expérimentale. C. R. Soc. Biol., Paris, 110:203–205.
1932b. Le *Trypanosoma cruzi* et ses rapports avec le système réticulo-endothélial. *Ibid.*, 110:206–210, 3 figs. in text.
1934. Persistance de l'infection par le *Schizotrypanum cruzi* chez l'Homme. *Ibid.*, 117:506–507.

DOMINICI, H.
1900a. Sur l'histologie de la rate normale. Arch. de Med. expér. et d'Anat. path., 12:563–588, 6 figs. in text.
1900b. Sur l'histologie de la rate au cours des états infectieux. *Ibid.*, 12:733–768, pls. 14–16, 4 figs. in text.
1901. Sur l'histologie de la rate à l'état normal et pathologique. *Ibid.*, 13:1–50, pls. 1–3, 5 figs. in text.
1921. Etudes sur le tissu conjonctif et les organes hématopoiétiques des mammifères. III. Modifications des organes hématopoiétiques. Arch. d'Anat. Microsc., 17: 247–301, pls. 22–30.

DOWNEY, H., and WEIDENREICH, F.
1912. Ueber die Bildung der Lymphocyten in Lymphdrüsen und Milz. IX. Fortsetzung der "Studien über das Blut und die blut-bildenden und -zerstörenden Organe." Arch. f. mikr. Anat., 80:306–395, pls. 16–18.

GALLIARD, H.
1929. Envahissement précoce et intense de la cavité abdominale chez le Souris au cours des infections à *Trypanosoma cruzi*. Ann. Parasit. humaine et comparée, 7:377–380.
1930. Localisation péritonéale exclusive au cours de certaines infections à *Trypanosoma cruzi* chez le Souris. Ann. Parasit. humaine et comparée, 8:140–142.

GEOGHEGAN, A.
1929. A propos d'un nouveau cas de trypanosomiase humaine américaine dans la ville de Catamarca. C. R. Soc. Biol., Paris, 100:137.

HARTMANN, A.
   1930. "Die Milz" *in* v. Möllendorff's Handbuch der mikroskopischen Anatomie des Menschen, 6:397–563, 60 figs. in text.

HOYER, H.
   1894. Ueber den Bau der Milz. Morphol. Arb., 3:229–300, pls. 11–12.

HU, C. H.
   1931. The lymphatic reaction in experimental trypanosomiasis. Nat. Med. Jour. China, 17:435–457, pls. 1–7.
   1933. Histopathology of kala-azar in experimentally infected hamsters, with special reference to plasma cells, myeloid tissue, reticulo-endothelial system, and reticulum fibers. Chinese Med. Jour., 47:1112–1124, pls. 1–13.
   1934. Studies on the mature and immature lymphoid cells of spleen, lymph nodes and thymus of normal rats and rats infected with *Trypanosoma brucei*. Am. Jour. Path., 10:29–42, pls. 39–41.

HU, C. H., and CASH, J. R.
   1929. Studies upon the peripheral blood, bone marrow and spleen of hamsters experimentally infected with kala-azar. Trans. of the F. E. A. T. M., 7th Cong., India, 3:62–76, pl. 3.

HU, C. H., and CH'IN, K. Y.
   1933. Development of lymphocytes and plasma cells in rats experimentally infected with trypanosomiasis. Proc. Soc. Exp. Biol. and Med., 30:435–436.

JAFFÉ, R. H.
   1921. Ueber die extramedullare Blutbildung bei anämischen Mäusen. Zieglers Beiträge, 68:224–257, pl. 10.
   1931. Anatomie und Pathologie der Spontanerkrankungen der kleinen Laboratoriumstiere (Berlin, Julius Springer), 832 pp., 270 figs. in text.

JAROTZKY, A.
   1908. Morphologische Veränderungen in der Milz nach der Infektion bei passiv immunisierten Tieren. Virch. Archiv., 191:112–135.

JOLLY, J.
   1923. Traité technique d'hæmatologie (Paris, Maloine et fils), 1131 pp., 1 pl., 699 figs. in text.

KLIENENBERGER, C., and CARL, W.
   1927. Die Blutmorphologie der Laboratoriumstiere (Leipzig, Barth), ed. 2, 136 pp., 7 pls.

KNOLL, W.
   1932. Das morphologische Blutbild der Säugetiere. I. Allgemeine und spezielle Morphologie der kernhaltigen Blutzellen der Säugetiere. Zeitschr. f. mikr. anat. Forsch., 30:116–150, pls. 4–5.

KOFOID, C. A., and DONAT, F.
   1933a. South American trypanosomiasis of the human type—occurrence in mammals in the United States. Calif. West. Med., 38:1–12, 5 figs. in text.
   1933b. Experimental infection with *Trypanosoma cruzi* from intestine of cone-nose bug, *Triatoma protracta*. Proc. Soc. Exp. Biol. and Med., 30:489–491.
   1933c. The experimental transfer of *Trypanosoma cruzi* from naturally infected *Triatoma protracta* to mammals in California. Bull. Soc. Path. Exot., 26:257–259.

LAVERAN, A.
   1908. Sur quelques altérations de la rate chez les Cobayes infectés de trypanosomes. Bull. Soc. Path. Exot., 1:393–398.

LOCATELLI, P.
   1929. Les mégacaryocytes des Cobayes trypanosomés. C. R. Soc. Biol., Paris, 101: 1048–1050.

LOEWENTHAL, N.
   1933. Observations sur les globules blancs du sang des Mammifères. Arch. d'Anat., d'Histol. et d'Embryol., 17:247–272, pl. 7.

1934. Des particularités des globules blancs non granules du sang chez le Campagnol et les Murides. *Ibid.*, 18:299–326, pl. 1.

MACROBERT, R. G.
1929. South American trypanosomiasis of the meningo-encephalomyelitic type in New York. Jour. Am. Med. Assoc., 92:230–231.

MARMORSTON-GOTTESMAN, J., PERLA, D., and VORZIMER, J.
1930. Immunological studies in relation to the suprarenal gland. VI*a*. *Trypanosoma lewisi* infection in normal albino rats. Jour. Exp. Med., 52:587–600.

MAXIMOW, A. A.
1909. Ueber zweckmassige Methoden fur zytologische und histogenetische Untersuchungen. Zeitschr. f. wiss. Mikrosk., 26:177–190.
1927. Morphology of the mesenchymal reactions. Arch. Path. and Lab. Med., 4:557–606.

MAXIMOW, A. A., and BLOOM, W.
1931. A text-book of histology (Philadelphia, Saunders), 833 pp., 604 figs. in text.

MAZZA, S.
1926*a*. Infection spontanée du Chien par le *Schizotrypanum cruzi*. C. R. Soc. Biol., Paris, 95:809–811.
1926*b*. Cas de trypanosomose humaine observé dans la ville de Jujuy. *Ibid.*, 95:815.
1930. Acerca de la infección espontánea de la mulita por el "*Trypanosoma cruzi*" en el Norte Argentina. Comprobación en el miocardio y pulmón de los "Gigantocitos quisticos" de Magarinos Torres (Segunda nota preliminar). Trop. Dis. Bull., 27:840 (abstract).

McCOY-HILL, F.
1930. Lymphoid hyperplasia in mice. Jour. Cancer Res., 14:325–358, 17 figs. in text.

MICHELS, N. A.
1931. The erythrocyte. Haematologica, Recensioni, 11:102–158.

NAEGELI, O.
1931. Blutkrankheiten und Blutdiagnostik (Berlin, Julius Springer), ed. 5, 704 pp., 104 figs. in text.

NIÑO, F. L.
1929. Contribución al Estudio de la Enfermedad de Chagas o Tripanosomiasis Americana en la Republica Argentina (Buenos Aires, Imprenta de la Universidad), 237 pp., 8 pls., 54 figs. in text.

PAPPENHEIM, A.
1907. Einige Bemerkungen über Methoden und Ergebnisse der sog. Vitalfärbung an den Erythrocyten. Fol. Haematol., Supplement, 4:46–53.
1911. Kurze technologische Zusammenstellung der Färbungsvorschriften mit Panchrom. *Ibid.*, 12:178–180.

PAPPENHEIM, A., and HIRSCHFELD, H.
1920. Haematologische Bestimmungstafeln (Leipzig, Klinkhardt), 335 pp., 6 pls.

PETRI, S.
1930. "Die Untersuchungsmethoden der hämatopoetischen Organe," *in* Hirschfeld and Hittmair's Handbuch der allgemeinen Hämatologie, 2:197–228.
1933. Morphologie und Zahl der Blutkörperchen bei 7-ca. 30 g. schweren normalen weissen Laboratoriumsmäusen. Acta Path. Scandinavica, 10:159–238, pl. 1.
1934. Morphologische und numerische Untersuchungen über Knockenmarkzellen bei normalen weissen Laboratoriumsmäusen. *Ibid.*, 11:1–43, pls. 1–2.

POINDEXTER, H. A.
1933. Observations on the defense mechanism in *Trypanosoma equiperdum* and *Trypanosoma lewisi* infections in guinea pigs and rats. Am. Jour. Trop. Med., 13:555–575.

SCARBOROUGH, R. A.
1930. The blood picture of normal laboratory animals. Yale Jour. Biol. and Med., 3:267–282.

SIMONDS, J. R.
    1925. Leukemia, pseudoleukemia and related conditions in the Slye stock of mice. Jour. Cancer Res., 9:329–373, 5 figs. in text.

SOUZA-CAMPOS, E. DE
    1929. Corpos intranucleares nos cellulos do reticulo endothelial do ganglio lymphatico parasitado pelo *Trypanosoma cruzi* (Nota prévia). Bol. Biol., no. 16:99–100, 2 figs. in text.

STITT, E. R.
    1927. Practical bacteriology, blood work and animal parasitology (Philadelphia, Blakiston), ed. 8, 837 pp., 1 pl., 211 figs. in text.

TORRES, C. M., and de AZEVEDO, A. P.
    1929a. Cellules géantes kystiques chez l'Armadille (*Dasypus novemcinctus* L.), qui présente l'infection spontanée par le *Trypanosoma cruzi* Chagas, 1909. C. R. Soc. Biol., Paris, 102:412–414, 2 figs. in text.
    1929b. Cellules géantes kystiques chez le Chien infecté expérimentalement par *Trypanosoma cruzi*, souche de l'Armadille. *Ibid.*, 102:416–418, 2 figs. in text.

VILLELA, E., and DIAS, EMMANUEL
    1934a. Sur la formation d'ulcérations chez les animaux infectés par le *Schizotrypanum cruzi*. C. R. Soc. Biol., Paris, 117:394–395.
    1934b. Localisation des formes de multiplication du *Schizotrypanum cruzi* dans la peau et dans les muqueuses de Chiens expérimentalement infectés. Parasitisme de la cellule épithéliale de l'épiderme. *Ibid.*, 117:501–504, 3 figs. in text.

WOOD, F. D.
    1934a. Experimental studies on *Trypanosoma cruzi* in California. Proc. Soc. Exp. Biol. and Med., 32:61–62.
    1934b. Natural and experimental infection of *Triatoma protracta* Uhler and mammals in California with American human trypanosomiasis. Am. Jour. Trop. Med., 14: 497–517, pls. 1–3.

ZUCCARINI, J. A.
    1930. Etudes expérimentales sur le *Trypanosoma cruzi*. C. R. Soc. Biol., Paris, 105: 113–115.

EXPLANATION OF PLATES

All figures of plate 20 were drawn by Dr. Fae D. Wood with the aid of a camera lucida, ×
2100. All cells, except the trypanosomes in figure 2, and figure 15, are from normal blood.
The cells in figures 1 and 3 were stained with Giemsa's blood stain after treatment with
Knoll's fixative, and benzidine solution; that in figure 4 was stained with Giemsa's blood
stain after treatment with Knoll's fixative, and benzidine and copper sulphate solutions.
All other cells were stained with May-Giemsa.

The photomicrographs of plates 21 and 22, which were made from slides stained with
Delafield's hematoxylin and eosin, were taken by Mr. J. E. Gullberg.

PLATE 20

Fig. 1. Multilobulated type neutrophil showing varying intensity of oxydase reaction in neutrophil granules (benzidine solution only).

Fig. 2. Red blood corpuscle, blood platelets, and *Trypanosoma cruzi*.

Fig 3. Type *a* eosinophil showing pronounced oxydase reaction (benzidine solution only).

Fig. 4. Segmented type *a* neutrophil after oxydase reaction (benzidine and copper sulphate solution).

Fig. 5. Multilobulated type neutrophil showing numerous granules.

Fig 6. Segmented type *a* neutrophil showing few granules.

Fig. 7. Segmented type *b* neutrophil showing many granules.

Fig. 8. Unsegmented type neutrophil showing few granules

Fig. 9. Type *a* eosinophil.

Fig. 10. Type *b* eosinophil.

Fig. 11. Type *a* basophil.

Fig. 12. Type *b* basophil.

Fig. 13. Mononuclear showing fine chromatin meshwork.

Fig. 14. Mononuclear showing coarse and fine chromatin meshwork.

Fig. 15. "Macrolymphocyte" from blood of mouse infected with *Trypanosoma cruzi*.

Fig. 16. Large lymphocyte with irregularly shaped nucleus.

Fig. 17. Small lymphocyte.

Fig. 18. Medium-sized lymphocyte with granular inclusions.

Fig. 19. Medium-sized lymphocyte.

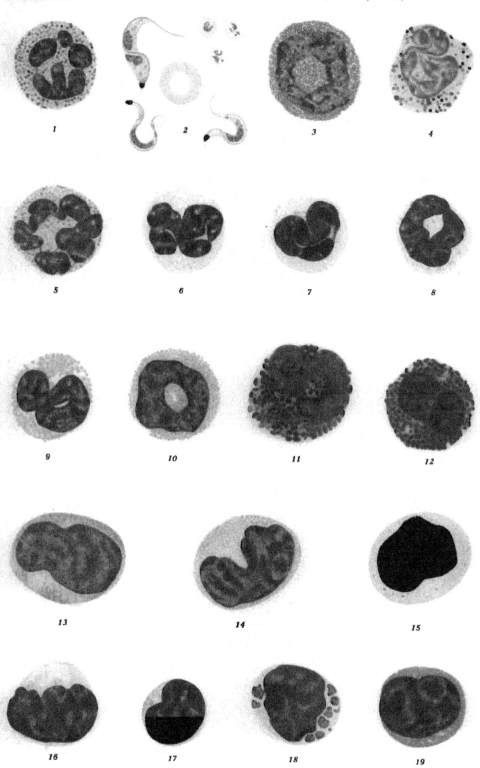

PLATE 21

Fig. 20. × 30. Spleen from 34-gram normal mouse, showing small size of follicles and distinct zonation of primary and secondary (germinal center) nodules. Note the extent of the interfollicular tissue and its appearance, owing to its low cellular content.

Fig. 21. × 30. Spleen from 33-gram infected mouse, showing increase in the size of the follicles tending toward obliteration of the primary nodules. Note the distinctness of the marginal zone surrounding the follicles and the sharp contrast with which this zone is set off from the interfollicular tissue. The scattered groups of developing erythroblasts, eosinophil myelocytes, small lymphocytes, and plasma cells give the blotchy appearance to the interfollicular tissue.

Fig. 22. × 30. Spleen from 50-gram infected mouse, showing enlargement of the follicles, with increased cellularity of the interfollicular tissue.

Fig. 23. × 275. Interfollicular tissue of the spleen of figure 20, showing scattered groups of deeply stained small cells (mostly erythroblasts).

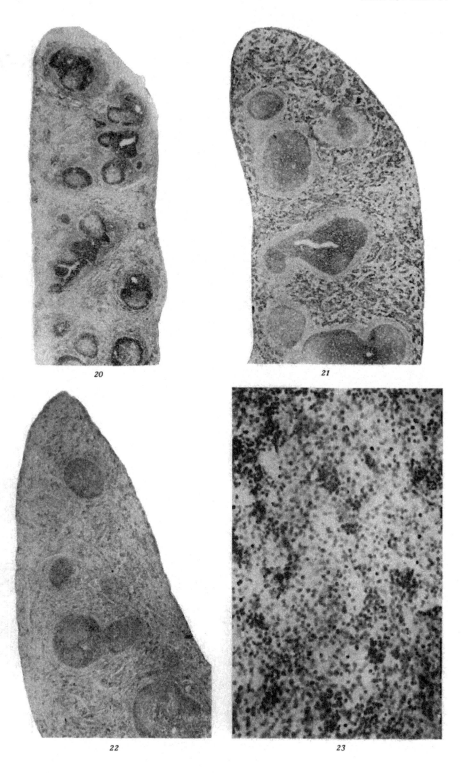

20

21

22

23

PLATE 22

Fig. 24. × 125. Follicle from spleen of 34-gram normal mouse, showing active germinal center (secondary nodule) completely surrounded by the primary nodule, which in turn is surrounded by a more or less distinct marginal zone which merges at various places with the interfollicular tissue.

Fig. 25. × 125. Follicle from spleen of 33-gram infected mouse, showing partial obliteration of the primary nodule owing to the great activity of the cells of the germinal center. Observe the distinct marginal zone sharply separated from both the primary nodule and the interfollicular tissue. Note the giant cells in the interfollicular tissue.

Fig. 26. × 530. Part of follicle of figure 24, showing character of the nuclei of cells of different zones, from the germinal center (top) to interfollicular tissue (bottom). Note the nuclei of medium-sized and large lymphocytes and of a few reticular cells in the germinal center, the deeply stained nuclei of the closely packed small lymphocytes of the primary nodule, and the nuclei of the small and medium-sized lymphocytes in the marginal zone. The borders of some sinuses are visible in the interfollicular tissue.

Fig. 27. × 530. Part of follicle of figure 25, showing character of the nuclei of cells of different zones, from the germinal center (top) to the interfollicular tissue (bottom). Note the few scattered cells of the primary nodule, the distinct broad marginal zone, and the increased cellular content of the interfollicular tissue.

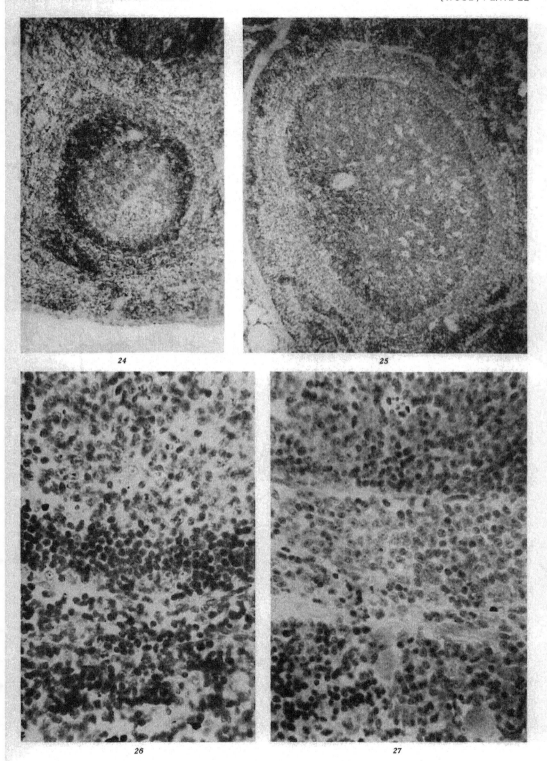

24

25

26

27

CPSIA information can be obtained
at www.ICGtesting.com
Printed in the USA
BVOW04s1500150817

492126BV00003B/6/P